DONALD B. KRAYBILL

SIMPLY AMISH

AN ESSENTIAL GUIDE
from the Foremost Expert on Amish Life

HERALD
PRESS

Harrisonburg, Virginia

Herald Press
PO Box 866, Harrisonburg, Virginia 22803
www.HeraldPress.com

The Library of Congress has cataloged the hardcover edition as follows:
Library of Congress Cataloging-in-Publication Data
Names: Kraybill, Donald B., author.
Title: Simply Amish : an essential guide from the foremost expert on Amish
    life / Donald B. Kraybill.
Other titles: Amish
Description: Harrisonburg : Herald Press, 2018. | Rev. ed. of: The Amish :
    why they enchant us. c2003.
Identifiers: LCCN 2018010811 | ISBN 9781513803296 (hardcover : alk. paper)
Subjects: LCSH: Amish--United States--Social life and customs..
Classification: LCC E184.M45 .K74 2018 | DDC 289.7/30973--dc23 LC record
available at https://lccn.loc.gov/2018010811

SIMPLY AMISH
© 2018 by Herald Press, Harrisonburg, Virginia 22803. 800-245-7894.
    All rights reserved.
Library of Congress Control Number: 2018010811
International Standard Book Number: 978-1-5138-0329-6 (hardcover);
    978-1-5138-0422-4 (paperback)
Printed in Canada
Cover and interior design by Reuben Graham
Cover photo by Willard / iStock / Thinkstock

Photo and graphic credits: Grant Beachy: 4–5, 26, 29, 30–31, 32, 45, 58, 59, 88; Cartarium / iStock / Thinkstock: 10; Dennis Hughes: 12, 50, 65, 79; Jan Luyken: 14; Lucian Niemeyer: 48; Daniel Rodriguez: 19, 20, 40, 51, 68, 72, 74, 83, 86, 93; Blair Seitz: 64, 76; Lucas Swartzentruber-Landis: 53, 60–61, 90, 94; Shirley Wenger: 77; Doyle Yoder: 7, 9, 16, 23, 37, 55, 80.

Unless otherwise indicated, all Scripture is taken from the *King James Version*, or *New Revised Standard Version*, © 1989, Division of Christian Education of the National Council of the Churches of Christ in the United States of America. Used by permission. All rights reserved.

All author royalties from this book are contributed to a nonprofit foundation for distribution to charitable causes.

Simply Amish is the revised edition of *The Amish: Why They Enchant Us*, published by Herald Press in 2003.

22 21 20 19 18   10 9 8 7 6 5 4 3 2 1

CONTENTS

AMISH CHARM

Lovely quilts, charming handicrafts, and fine oak furniture. Stunning flower gardens, colorful laundry on outdoor lines, and horses plodding across rural landscapes.

For anyone traveling in "Amish Country" such images may hearken back to life in colonial America, when people read by candlelight, washed clothing by hand, and traveled by horseback. With their distinctive dress, language, and lifestyle, the Amish are one of North America's more fascinating ethnic communities. They have stubbornly refused to be swallowed up by contemporary culture. Yet idyllic images of Amish life may deceive us into thinking the Amish are social antiques, frozen in time. How, we wonder, do they resist modern encroachments from creeping into their communities and tearing them asunder?

If quizzed about Amish life, most people might know that the Amish travel by horse and buggy and wear peculiar dress. But beyond the beards, bonnets, and buggies, many people know little. Do the Amish pay taxes? Do they prearrange marriages? Do they live in cloistered communities, use modern medicine, worship in church buildings, speak English, and attend high school? Where do they find a Bible verse that forbids motor vehicles? Do they really shun all modern technology? Is divorce permitted in their communities? And what about *Rumspringa*: do Amish youth truly run wild, or is that just a myth perpetrated by reality TV shows like *Amish Mafia*? Perhaps most importantly: are Amish communities holding their own or dying out?

What are the secrets of Amish success, the sources of their wisdom? And why do these stubborn traditionalists enchant us? Perhaps their sense of place, their social stability, and their audacity to buck modern culture intrigue us. Amid the stress and press of contemporary life, we are curious how they retain stable communities and strong social bonds. Their sense of simplicity, frugality, and apparent contentment with fewer things and a slower pace of life also lure us. How do they find satisfaction without televisions, video games, social media, and cars?

A group of Amish women and children enjoy wading in a stream.

In this book we'll explore these questions, debunk some myths, and pose some provocative questions about our relationship with our Amish neighbors. I have researched and written about the Amish for more than forty years, and my Amish friends have graciously helped me to both understand their way of life and ask questions about my own.

Perhaps our enchantment with the Amish belies our own discontentment with modern life. We may not always agree with them, yet we admire their courage to practice their faith in the face of high-tech life, driven by relentless change. The Amish may be good for stirring warm, nostalgic feelings about an imagined American past; but do they offer any wisdom for the rest of us living a full-throated modern life?

GROWTH AND DIVERSITY

We might expect a group that rejects higher education and advanced technology to be dying. Surprisingly, the Amish are growing. Their population doubles about every twenty years. Counting adults and children, they number more than 325,000

Right: More than 85 percent of children raised in an Amish home will join the church and remain Amish throughout their lives. This father is a member of an Amish group that has more traditional styles of dress and haircuts than many Amish communities.

souls. One Amish woman joked, "If we keep growing so fast, soon half the world will be Amish and the other half will be 'taxi drivers' who haul us around." So how do the Amish manage to not merely survive but actually thrive in the midst of modern life?

Distribution of Amish congregations in North America

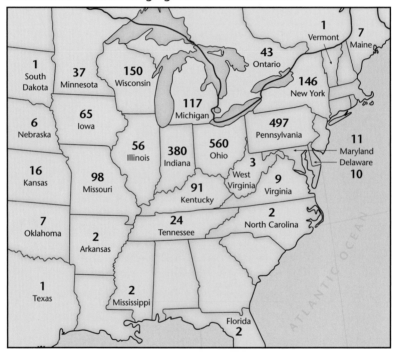

The Amish live in thirty-one states and several Canadian provinces. A search for affordable farmland has propelled many new settlements in recent years.

Note: Additional congregations in Colorado (5), Montana (9), Prince Edward Island (2), Idaho (1), New Brunswick (1), and Wyoming (1).

Source: "Amish Population, 2017." Young Center for Anabaptist and Pietist Studies, Elizabethtown College. http://groups.etown.edu/amishstudies/statistics/population-2017/.

Large families and strong retention rates propel Amish growth. On the average, families have about seven children, but it's not unusual to have ten or more. Typically, about 85 percent of Amish youth join the church but in some communities, retention rises above 95 percent. Although the Amish do not evangelize or seek converts, outsiders may join if they comply with Amish guidelines. Several dozen "English," as outsiders are called, have entered the Amish flock in recent decades, but that's a small number.

Amish people reside in more than five hundred settlements in thirty-one states, mostly east of the Mississippi. Some also live in several Canadian provinces. The three most populous states are Ohio, Pennsylvania, and Indiana. New communities form yearly, while others flounder and die. The two largest Amish settlements—in Holmes County, Ohio, and Lancaster County, Pennsylvania—each claim more than two hundred congregations. In stark contrast, about half the settlements have just one congregation. North America has some 2,400 Amish congregations, each of which typically has twenty-five to thirty-five households.

This book focuses on Amish groups that use horse-and-buggy transportation. Two other groups with Amish roots (Beachy Amish and Amish Mennonites) own automobiles, use electricity from the public grid, and engage more with outsiders than the buggy-driving Amish.

At first glance, the horse-and-buggy Amish all look alike. Dig deeper and you will discover more than three dozen subgroups that

The identity of diverse Amish groups is reflected in the color of their buggies. Each church group specifies the color and style of their buggies. Some of the carriage bodies are made from wood, others from fiberglass, and in some communities, from plastic.

populate the Amish world. Each of these "tribes," so to speak, has its own unique practices. Some, for example, have black-topped carriages, while other tribes sport gray, white, yellow, or burnt orange tops. The subgroups vary as to their use of technology, views of women, interaction with outsiders, interpretations of the Bible, and guidelines for their youth. Some communities are wealthy, and others are rather poor. These tribes are scattered across a wide continuum from traditional to progressive. To illustrate their differences, I frequently mention the ends of the spectrum. In reality, however, most Amish subgroups don't fit neatly into those two boxes.

Even so, all the Amish share a separatist identity and a common history. The Amish story stretches back nearly five centuries, to the sixteenth-century Protestant Reformation in Europe.

Amish Roots

The Amish trace their religious roots to a radical movement that emerged in Zürich, Switzerland, in 1525 and soon spread to other regions of Europe. These "heretics," as they were considered by others, refused to baptize babies. They insisted that only adults who had voluntarily decided to follow the teachings of Jesus should be baptized. So they rebaptized each other as adults.

The opponents of the radicals soon called them Anabaptists, or "rebaptizers," a derogatory nickname. The Anabaptists sought to practice the teachings of Jesus in daily life, and they placed allegiance to the Bible above the dictates of civil government. Surprisingly, they were early proponents of two important modern ideas: the separation of church and state, and adult choice in religion.

Infant baptism in sixteenth-century Europe bestowed four things on a child: citizenship, church membership, an entry on tax rolls, and a spot on conscription lists. For these reasons, the Anabaptists were deemed not only religious heretics but anarchists who threatened to wreak havoc on the political order. Their defiant acts were a capital crime in a society in which Protestant churches, the Roman Catholic Church, and civil law all *required* babies to be baptized.

The Anabaptists outraged civil and religious authorities, who thought the radicals would shred the centuries-old fabric of church and state. The severe persecution of the Anabaptists, beginning in

1527, continued for many years. Hundreds were executed. They were torched at the stake, drowned in lakes, tortured in public spectacles, and starved in dungeons. A twelve-hundred-page book, *The Bloody Theater, or Martyrs Mirror of the Defenseless Christians*, records many stories of their abysmal fate. Even today, many Amish families have a copy of the *Martyrs Mirror* in their homes. Ministers recount stories from it in their sermons, reminding members that even today they are pilgrims and strangers in this world of woe.

The harsh persecution drove many Swiss Anabaptists into hiding in rural areas. This galvanized their belief that their church community should stand apart from mainstream culture. Separation from the world, sometimes called nonconformity, soon became a key tenet of faith. This idea was underscored by verses in the New Testament such as "Love not the world, neither the things that are in the world" (1 John 2:15) and "Be not conformed to this world" (Romans 12:2).

The Amish emerged in 1693 as a distinctive group among Swiss Anabaptists and among some who had fled Swiss persecution for the Alsace region of southeastern France. Jakob Ammann, a recent convert who became an Anabaptist leader, sought to reinvigorate church life, which he thought had stagnated in the nearly 170 years since the birth of Anabaptism in Zürich. Other Swiss Anabaptist

Left: *Martyrs Mirror* includes stories of the ancestors of the Amish who were martyred for their faith. Here, the son of martyr Jacob Dircks embraces him as he is led to his death in 1568.

Separation from the world, or nonconformity, became a key part of Amish faith centuries ago. That separation is maintained today in part by distinctive dress for both women and men.

leaders did not welcome his ideas. Ammann argued for a sharper separation from the Swiss Reformed Church, and among other changes, he called for shunning (excommunication and exclusion) of wayward members to keep the church pure. This was not a new idea. It was an older Catholic practice that some German Pietists also endorsed during Ammann's time.

These cleavages among the Swiss Anabaptists led to a division in 1693. Ammann's followers were soon called Amish. The remaining Anabaptists were known as Swiss Brethren. Eventually they, as well as Anabaptists in Germany, became known as

Mennonites. This name derived from Menno Simons, a prominent Dutch Anabaptist leader who had converted to Anabaptism in 1536 and whose writings had influenced Anabaptists in various parts of western Europe.

AMISH AND MENNONITES

Some Amish people came to North America in the mid-1700s, and others in the 1800s. They formed communities in Pennsylvania, Ohio, and Indiana and eventually spread to other states, often settling near their spiritual cousins, the Mennonites. The last Amish congregation in Europe closed in 1937. In the twenty-first century today, about 95 percent of all Amish people reside in the United States; the other 5 percent live in Canada.

In vivid contrast, Mennonites in the twenty-first century live in eighty-seven different countries on six continents, including Europe and North America. More than 60 percent of the global Mennonite family lives in Africa, Asia, and Latin America. In fact, the numbers suggest that the typical Mennonite today is an African woman. Mennonite populations dispersed through various migrations and through missionary and service efforts. Mennonites in the United States claim sixty different subgroups and a total population of about 400,000.

Like the Amish, some Mennonites use horse-and-buggy transportation—but only about 5 percent of Mennonites do. These Old Order Mennonites share other traits with the Amish as well. Some of the similarities include speaking Pennsylvania German, attending one-room schools, terminating schooling at eighth grade, and wearing distinctive dress. Both churches reject Sunday school and evangelistic outreach. The two groups cooperate in numerous projects for Plain people, as they are sometimes called.

Several differences set the Old Order Mennonites and Amish apart. Mennonite buggies have different styles and colors than Amish ones. Unlike the Amish, Mennonite men do not wear beards. The dresses worn by Mennonite women typically have patterns, whereas Amish dresses rarely do. Mennonite farmers use steel-wheeled tractors in their fields, but the overwhelming majority of Amish farmers pull their machinery by horses. Finally, a big difference between Amish and Mennonites involves church. Mennonites worship in meetinghouses, while the Amish meet in homes. In contrast to the congregational authority of the Amish, the Old Order Mennonites have a centralized authority, which produces uniformity in different Mennonite settlements.

The remaining 95 percent of Mennonites in the United States who do not drive horses and buggies roughly fall into two clusters: conservative and assimilated. Members of *conservative* groups drive cars but have retained some traditional and separatist practices. On the other hand, *assimilated* Mennonites, who also drive cars, have largely discarded traditional ways of life.

Conservative Mennonites typically accept more technology and education than do the Amish. Still, these Mennonites share Amish convictions for wearing distinctive dress, nonparticipation in politics, rejecting divorce, not ordaining women, and selecting untrained lay ministers from within their congregations. Unlike the Amish, conservative Mennonites emphasize individual conversion, written doctrinal statements, and evangelism.

A gray Amish buggy follows a black Old Order Mennonite buggy in Lancaster, Pennsylvania.

Assimilated Mennonites have few separatist practices. The vast majority wear contemporary clothing, support higher education, use modern technology, and actively participate in mainstream culture. Many hold professional jobs, including some in the arts, the sciences, and the corporate world. Some of their congregations use musical instruments and creative dance to enhance worship. They are involved in peacemaking and social justice activities through national and global Mennonite and non-Mennonite

Assimilated Mennonites stand apart from the Amish, as well as from Old Order and conservative Mennonites, in their approach to dress, education, technology, and professions. Despite their differences, Mennonites and Amish sometimes collaborate in disaster relief and service projects.

organizations. A few are active in local, state, and national politics. In these ways, assimilated Mennonites stand apart from the Amish as well as from Old Order and conservative Mennonites.

Even so, the Amish and Mennonites share Anabaptist roots, adult baptism, a focus on the New Testament, and a discipleship theology that asks what it means to follow Jesus in daily life. Each group, however, answers that question in quite different ways. All the groups emphasize peacemaking, although not all members of assimilated congregations are conscientious objectors to war. Members of various groups join together for historical projects and participate in various Mennonite-organized service and disaster relief organizations that assist non-Anabaptists who are victims of flooding, hurricanes, or other natural disasters.

A Church with Boundaries

Amish families who live near each other form a local congregation called a church district. Each district has exact boundaries: creeks, roads, or township lines. About twenty five to thirty-five families live in a typical district. Households attend church services in the district in which they reside. If a family wants to join a different district, they must move to it. The church district is the social and religious hub of Amish life.

Members of each district meet for worship every other Sunday at one of their homes. The services, which rotate from home to home, often involve 150 or more children and adults. After a three-hour worship service, members enjoy a light fellowship lunch followed by visiting in the house or on the lawn. On their "free Sunday," members attend services in another district or spend a quiet day at home. When districts grow too big to meet in a home, they divide. In sparse Amish settlements, a district may stretch across fifteen miles or more. In densely populated ones, families may live within a mile of each other and walk to church services.

Each district has three types of leaders: a bishop, two ministers, and a deacon. The leaders, who are all men, are selected by drawing lots from nominees named by the congregation. Leaders serve for life without formal training or pay. The bishop is the spiritual head of the congregation. He officiates at baptisms, weddings, communions, confessions, congregational meetings, and funerals. He also interprets and enforces the regulations of the district. Besides preaching, the ministers assist with various leadership responsibilities. The deacon helps the bishop with disciplinary issues and cares for any economic needs of members.

The church district plays a prominent role in Amish life. It serves as church, club, precinct, and neighborhood all bundled together. Districts in spiritual fellowship with each other exchange

Right: In many church districts, members walk to religious services that meet every other Sunday in nearby homes. Horse-and-buggy transportation, as well as walking, encourages face-to-face relationships.

ministers, support similar regulations, and permit their members to intermarry. The Amish do not have church buildings, mission agencies, or religious organizations—not even a central national church office. Members are linked together through loose bonds of fellowship rather than by bureaucratic structures.

The twelve largest Amish communities

Settlement	State	Districts	Est. population
Lancaster County	Pennsylvania	220	36,920
Holmes County	Ohio	274	35,130
Elkhart/LaGrange Counties	Indiana	181	24,205
Geauga County	Ohio	132	18,650
Adams County	Indiana	58	8,595
Nappanee	Indiana	43	5,910
Daviess County	Indiana	29	4,855
Arthur	Illinois	30	4,410
Mifflin County	Pennsylvania	30	3,905
Allen County	Indiana	22	3,190
Indiana County	Pennsylvania	21	2,985
Seymour County	Missouri	16	2,665

The Amish have some 500 settlements and 2,400 church districts in North America. Settlements may spill over into adjacent counties. The twelve largest settlements are based on the number of church districts. The number of members per district varies in different settlements.

Religious Services and Rituals

Amish youth typically are baptized between age sixteen and their early twenties. Candidates are instructed in the Dordrecht Confession of Faith, an Anabaptist statement from 1632 that includes traditional doctrines of the Christian church (creation, sin, salvation, final judgment, and eternal life). At baptism, youth renounce the devil and the world, pledge their belief in Christ, and promise to obey the church for the rest of their lives. This solemn vow, with its lifelong consequences, makes baptism a pivotal turning point. A few youth elect not to join, but the vast majority of young adults surrender their lives to the church forever. Youth who have dabbled with worldly things abruptly turn their backs on them at baptism.

Amish worship services are not open to the public. However, the family who hosts a worship service sometimes will invite English neighbors or special friends to attend. I have been fortunate to attend many services. It was there, for the first time, that I grasped the deep core of Amish faith. The entire service is radically countercultural.

Holding worship services in homes reflects the simplicity and plainness of Amish life. There are no organs, guitars, stained glass windows, sound systems, pulpits, coffee bars, children's church, or Sunday school classes. Everyone worships together, in a large room, which underscores the oneness of the congregation. Extremely slow unison singing in German, without rhythm or instruments, unites the worshipers together. A single song can stretch on for more than twenty minutes. The ancient tunes are sung by memory. The words, many written by Anabaptist prisoners, are printed in the *Ausbund*, the Amish hymnal. The slow cadence of the hymns with their ancient words transports participants, in tone and mood, into a stark medieval world.

An opening sermon of roughly thirty minutes is followed by the main sermon, which lasts about an hour. The ordained leaders decide which one of them will preach during a private meeting at the beginning of the service while the congregation sings the opening hymn. The preachers speak extemporaneously, in Pennsylvania

Amish church services include songs from the *Ausbund*, (1564) a hymnal that contains German lyrics but no music.

German, without notes. In an opening rite of humility, they emphasize how unworthy and unqualified they are to speak.

Most remarkably, two- to five-year-old children sit patiently on wooden benches beside their parents for nearly three hours. A few of them quietly play with tiny toys. A small snack for children is passed midway through the service. Children who are able to walk sometimes toddle back and forth between their parents, who are seated on opposite sides of the room. Although mothers tend to the babies, fathers actively help to care for children during the service.

Fall and spring communion services rejuvenate both personal faith and the bonds of community. In a self-examination service two weeks before communion, members confess their sins publicly and reaffirm their commitment to the regulations of the church. If all is well, the congregation celebrates their renewed faith in a six-hour communion service that includes footwashing, as taught by Jesus. Unlike many Protestant celebrations of communion, which primarily focus on an individual's *personal* relationship with God, Amish communion also underscores the importance of right relationships in *community*. In fact, if dissension arises, communion may be delayed.

Amish people sometime stray into sin and deviance. Those who violate a major teaching of the church—flying in an airplane, filing a lawsuit, working in a bar, purchasing commercial insurance, cheating in business—will be asked to make a public confession at a congregational meeting. Those who refuse or defy the authority of the church may face excommunication.

Shunning typically follows excommunication. On the basis of biblical teaching (such as 1 Corinthians 5:3-5 and other passages), shunning has been practiced by various religious groups over the centuries. The Amish version involves public rituals of shaming to remind the wayward of their sin and nudge them back into fellowship. Although personal contact with ex-members does not necessarily end, regular members may not receive rides or goods from offenders or sit with them during public meals at reunions, weddings, funerals, or other social events. Expulsion is a heavy matter because it can lead to a lifetime of estrangement from family and friends.

Happily, those who do fall from grace can always return to the fold if they are willing to confess their wrongs and mend their ways. If that happens, shunning ceases. Young adults who leave the community having not been baptized are not excommunicated or shunned.

Shunning sounds harsh to modern ears. The Amish point out, however, that adult baptism rests on free choice, and the church door stands ajar for wayward souls who want to rejoin the church. Still, shunning makes baptism a weighty decision for young people. Are they willing to forever place their life under the authority of the church?

Right: Amish church services are held in homes, barns or large shops. Benches and copies of the *Ausbund* are set up in this basement for a service. Later they will be transported in a covered "bench wagon" to the next home that will host the service.

SPIRITUALITY AND CONVICTIONS

It's tempting for outsiders to fixate on the cultural expressions of Amish life—the beards, the quilts, the buggies, and the one-room schools. These public symbols set the Amish apart and make them interesting. Yet beneath the cultural surface throbs a rich spirituality. Hidden from public eye rests a unique set of religious convictions, which undergird the Amish way of life.

Amish spirituality is rooted in the teachings of Jesus, especially his Sermon on the Mount (Matthew 5–7). Amish people use Martin Luther's German translation of the Bible (1534). Although preachers make frequent references to the Old Testament, only New Testament texts are read in church. A passage from Matthew, Luke, or John is read in twenty-two of the twenty-six services throughout the year (with church held every other Sunday). Moreover, the readings from Matthew equal those from Luke and John combined. Plus, Matthew's three chapters on the Sermon on the Mount receive the most attention. The frequent use of Jesus' sermon makes it an Amish manifesto of faith, so to speak.

These examples from Matthew show some of the links between Amish spirituality and Jesus' Sermon on the Mount.

Left: Amish faith emphasizes humility and self-denial. Modest dress is seen as a way to guard against pride. Amish women wear a devotional covering, but the styles vary from group to group.

- "Blessed are the meek" (5:5) accents the importance of humility.
- "Blessed are the peacemakers" (5:9) and "Love your ene-mies" (5:44) undergird the Amish emphasis on nonviolence and conscientious objection to war.
- Being "salt" and "light" in the world (5:13, 14) inspires the Amish to practice their faith rather than to seek converts.
- Giving alms "in secret" (6:4) is the reason they do not collect public offerings in their church services but urge members to make private donations.
- "Judge not" (7:1) underscores humility and leads the Amish not to judge or condemn other religious groups.
- "Enter through the narrow gate; for the gate is wide and the road is easy that leads to destruction" (7:13) highlights the Amish emphasis on separation from worldly culture.
- "By their fruits ye shall know them" (7:20) encourages Amish people to focus on practicing their faith and obeying the teach-ings of Jesus in daily life rather than on highbrow doctrine.

Other key themes in Amish spirituality include self-denial, which one Amish man described as "sacrificing our own selfish interests and desires in our service to God." This notion—which flies in the face of "selfies" and the modern emphasis on self-achievement—originates in Jesus' words: "If any want to become my followers, let them deny themselves and take up their cross daily and follow me" (Luke 9:23).

The Amish emphasis on humility and self-denial leads them to abhor pride. They cite a host of biblical references that eschew pride, such as the proverb which underscores that the Lord hates "a proud look" (Proverbs 6:17). In Amish eyes, pride signals unfettered individualism. Actions that call attention to the self—such as showy clothing, wristwatches, fancy drapes, or even ornaments on a harness—are seen as exhibiting pride. Prohibitions against cosmetics, jewelry, and personal photographs also help to thwart pride. Amish people rarely permit their names or photographs to be used in news media. Children are taught these things via mottos, such as the reminder that *i* is the middle letter of *pride*. The word *joy* reminds children that *J*esus is first, *O*thers are next, and *Y*ou are last.

Amish faith also calls members to obedience to the will of God and to the teachings of Jesus. Members are taught to obey those with authority over them: children their parents, students their teachers, members their leaders, and younger ministers their bishop. Everyone is expected to obey the will of God as discerned and taught by the congregation. During members meetings under the guidance of ordained leaders, Amish men and women decide the district's regulations. They take seriously the promise in Matthew 18:18-20 that whatever you decide on earth will be bound in heaven, as well as the assurance that God is present wherever two or three are gathered in God's name. To Amish ears these passages imply that decisions made in the members meetings have divine endorsement. In this way, sanctioned by providence, church regulations become difficult to change. The ultimate religious authority, for the Amish, rests in the congregation's interpretation of Scripture and God's will.

Humility also shapes the Amish view of salvation. Rather than emphasizing emotional experiences and the assurance of salvation, Amish leaders speak of a "living hope": an abiding belief that God, a fair and righteous judge, will grant eternal life to the faithful followers of Jesus. Thus, they refrain from evangelical language of having a "personal relationship with Jesus" and being "born again," which emphasize individual experience. In a spirit of humility, they trust in God's providence for their salvation, believing that it flows from obedient living in the community of faith.

The heart of Amish spirituality involves yielding oneself to a higher authority. The Amish speak of "giving themselves up" to the church. Rather than bold, assertive individualism, they believe that submission—yielding to the will of God and to others—brings contentment. It is at this point that Amish society most sharply diverges from contemporary culture.

Children are taught the meaning of submission in the lines of a schoolroom verse:

> I must be a Christian child
> Gentle, patient, meek, and mild;
> Must be honest, simple, true
> In my words and actions too.
> I must cheerfully obey,
> Giving up my will and way.

Despite their strong emphasis on humility, obedience, and community, the Amish express respect for the dignity of each person. Within the moral boundaries of Amish life, members have many avenues to express their individual preferences. Even so, the community takes precedence over the individual. The welfare of the community ranks above individual rights and choices. Communal

Amish children are schooled in humility, obedience, and community. They grow up learning that yielding to God and to others brings contentment.

wisdom, accumulated over the decades, is valued more than the opinion of one person. On some matters, traditional beliefs are esteemed above scientific findings.

An excellent summary of Amish spirituality appears in "Rules of a Godly Life" ("Regeln eines Gottseligen Lebens"), first printed in 1736 in Switzerland. Amish minister Joseph Stoll translated it from German to English. The last paragraph of this widely read devotional essay contains this admonition: "Finally, in your conduct be friendly toward everyone and a burden to none. Toward God, live a holy life; toward yourself, be moderate; toward your fellow men, be fair; in life, be modest; in your manner, courteous; in admonition, friendly; in forgiveness, willing; in your promises, true; in your speech, wise; and out of a pure heart gladly share of the bounties you receive."

FORGIVENESS AT NICKEL MINES

Amish spirituality was severely tested when Charles Carl Roberts IV entered the West Nickel Mines Amish school in Lancaster County, Pennsylvania, in October 2006. He carried three guns, ammunition, and various supplies into the one-room school. The school, which had no phone, was not near a private residence.

Roberts took the teacher and the twenty-six children, ages six to thirteen, hostage. After the teacher escaped to call the police, Roberts dismissed the boys and barricaded himself and the remaining ten girls in the schoolroom. After tying their ankles together as they lay facedown on the floor, he methodically shot them execution style—killing five and seriously wounding the others. When the police stormed the school, he killed himself. Four of the surviving girls recovered well enough to live a normal life. Years later, the fifth survivor responds to communication but requires continuous care.

Roberts, a non-Amish neighbor, hauled milk from dairy farms (Amish and non-Amish) to a milk processing plant. He had no history of hostility toward Amish people. In a letter he left for his wife, he blamed his actions on his anger at God for the death of his firstborn infant daughter nine years earlier. Roberts and his wife had three other children.

Within seven hours of the tragedy, several Amish people went to Roberts's widow, her family, and Roberts's parents to extend words of compassion, grace, and forgiveness. Other Amish people publicly expressed words of forgiveness. The Amish response shocked the world.

Within a week, some 2,400 stories about Amish forgiveness appeared in media outlets around the world. The stunning speed of forgiveness, coming so shortly after the tragedy, transformed this tale of grace in a rural hamlet into an international story. The publicity perplexed the Amish. "It's just standard Christian forgiveness," said one Amish man. "It's just what Christians do every day. Why are all the news people making such a big deal of it?"

The forgiveness was spontaneous. The leaders of the Amish community didn't need to meet first—as one bishop told me, it was a "decided issue. It's just part of our history, part of our beliefs; it's what Jesus teaches us to do." From this leader's perspective, forgiveness was in their spiritual DNA. Still, it wasn't easy to lay aside resentment and revenge. Even five months after the shooting, an Amish man confided, "Every morning when I get up, I have to start all over again with forgiveness."

The Nickel Mines Amish tore down the old school building and built a new one nearby. The New Hope school opened six months after the tragedy.

In some ways, the Amish response was more about compassion and grace than forgiveness. One Amish man told me, "The Roberts family had a much heavier burden [of shame] to carry than we did." Amish people clearly understood that Roberts, who had no history of mental illness, was very disturbed.

A father who lost a daughter in the school and had a second one seriously injured said, "Our forgiveness was more about what we *did* than what we *said*." Forgiveness was embodied in concrete acts, such as financial gifts to Roberts's widow and her three children. When Roberts was buried beside his firstborn daughter in a public cemetery, more than half the people who attended the burial service were Amish. Some of them had buried their own daughters just a day before. Despite that, they embraced Roberts's widow and other members of his family in a dramatic symbol of forgiveness.

When I asked Amish people in the Nickel Mines community why they forgive, they pointed, without exception, to the Lord's Prayer, in which Jesus taught his disciples to pray: "Forgive us the wrongs we have done, as we have forgiven those who have wronged us." One bishop emphasized that forgiveness is the *only* part of the Lord's Prayer that Jesus underscored. "Look at the two verses at the end of the prayer," he said. "They are very clear: if you don't forgive, you won't be forgiven by the Lord" (see Matthew 6:14-15).

Children learn the Lord's Prayer by memory at an early age, and it is used frequently in family devotions and at every church service. Amish people also cite other Bible verses that highlight the centrality of forgiveness in the Christian faith.

The Amish understood that forgiveness has two dimensions: emotional and behavioral. The emotional aspect involves letting go of grudges, resentment, and bitterness. The behavioral part means forgoing retaliation. In the face of injustice, the universal human impulse seeks to strike back and get even. A father who lost a daughter in the schoolhouse shooting defined forgiveness as "giving up my right to revenge."

Amish people also make a distinction between forgiveness and pardon. When asked what should have happened to Roberts if he were still alive, Amish people told me they thought he should be in prison so he wouldn't hurt other children. They would forgive him—that is, not hold bitterness or anger against him—but they couldn't pardon him, or erase his punishment. That was the job of the state. Justice would be served, in Amish eyes, if he was held accountable and incarcerated to protect other innocent children.

For the Amish, forgiveness is ritualized twice a year, in a council meeting two weeks before the communion service. The meeting focuses on forgiveness as a way to resolve conflicts in the congregation. The communion service is viewed as a celebration of the congregation's unity. If a congregation can't achieve unity, communion is postponed for several weeks or longer if needed, which adds a ritual incentive to forgive.

The prominence of the Lord's Prayer in Amish liturgy, their emphasis on biblical stories of forgiveness, and their biannual rituals of council meetings and communion services: all these things thread forgiveness throughout the fabric of Amish life. These practices foster a predisposition toward forgiveness, which was so tenderly demonstrated in the wake of the Nickel Mines tragedy.

EXPECTATIONS FOR DAILY LIVING

A mish people are always in church," Karen Johnson-Weiner, one of my colleagues, often notes. She doesn't mean this literally, of course, but as a way to describe the fact that church regulations cast a wide influence over Amish life. Amish values are translated into guidelines for daily living called the *Ordnung*, a German word that means "order." The *Ordnung* is a set of regulations, or expectations, for daily living. Usually unwritten, the rules are passed on by practice and oral tradition. They are updated as new issues arise. Children learn the rules by observation. Many expectations—the taboos against mustaches, divorce, television, and military service—need little discussion, because they are simply taken for granted. More controversial issues—such as cell phones, computers, fancy lawn ornaments, or fashionable dress— are discerned in members meetings.

Members of each congregation affirm the *Ordnung* twice a year before the spring and fall communion services. The details of the *Ordnung* vary by subgroup as well as by local congregation. For example, many Amish groups permit the use of propane gas stoves and refrigerators, but some do not. Most Amish homes have indoor bathrooms and plumbing, but members of the most traditional tribes walk to the outhouse. The *Ordnung*, said one person, is "an agreement among our members about how we should live." The words of a minister echo this belief: "If members respect the *Ordnung*, it generates peace, love, contentment, equality, and unity." Even so, disagreements over the details of the *Ordnung* can at times become quite contentious.

The *Ordnung* defines expectations and taboos for conduct ranging from personal dress to the use of technology. All Amish subgroups expect men and women to wear distinctive clothing. Married men are expected to grow a beard and wear an Amish-style hat and vest. Women wear a head covering and usually a three-piece dress that includes a cape and an apron. The details of color and style vary from group to group. Unlike mainstream culture, in which dress is a tool of individual adornment, in Amish life it signals submission to the collective order and serves as a public symbol of group identity. Members are expected to adhere to the dress standards of their tribe.

As part of their *Ordnung*, most Amish groups forbid owning automobiles; tapping electricity from the public grid; using self-propelled farm machinery; having a television, radio, or computer; attending high school and college; joining the military; and initiating divorce.

Right: Amish dress signals humility and submission to the church and limits individual choice.

Some things, like speaking Pennsylvania German, are just taken for granted. Even though Pennsylvania German is not part of the *Ordnung*, it's expected to be on the lips of everyone. This is the first language a child learns. It is spoken every day in family life, on the farm, in business, and wherever Amish people congregate. They quickly shift to English whenever an outsider appears. Religious documents, including hymnbooks, are usually written and read in German, but Amish people typically write English for day-to-day notes, letters, and other written communications within their own community.

Schools and Scholars

It may surprise some people to learn that before 1950, Amish children attended public schools. Indeed, some Amish fathers served as directors of rural public schools. They were comfortable with the small one- or two-room rural schools controlled by nearby neighbors. After World War II, many public schools began requiring attendance until age sixteen. About the same time, clusters of small schools—consolidated into large buildings in big geographical districts—replaced the iconic one-room school. Some Amish parents protested these developments, because they were losing control over the nurture of their children. They also considered "book learning" and study beyond the eighth grade unnecessary to prepare youth for a successful Amish life.

In some states, Amish parents sat in prison for refusing to send their children to public high schools. For two decades, several states pressed charges against the Amish. Finally, in 1972, the U.S. Supreme Court, in the decision *Wisconsin v. Yoder*, ruled that Amish children could end their formal schooling at eighth grade. The court concluded that "a way of life that is odd or even erratic but interferes with no rights or interests of others is not to be condemned because it is different."

Today, a few Amish children still attend rural public schools, but the vast majority go to one- or two-room schools operated by Amish parents. An estimated 60,000 Amish youth attend some 2,200 private schools that end with eighth grade. Instruction occurs in English. For some scholars, as Amish students are called, school is their first exposure to English. The teachers are typically self-trained Amish women who have not gone to high school but are graduates of Amish schools themselves. Educated through periodic teachers' meetings, by respected mentors, and through the *Blackboard Bulletin*, an Amish teachers' magazine, Amish teachers are selected for their teaching ability and their embrace of Amish values.

Usually, three to five male trustees maintain the school and hire the teacher. Parents pay tuition to support the schools. (In some states parents also pay taxes to support public schools.) One teacher may be responsible for instructing all eight grades, or in a two-room school, the grades may be divided between two

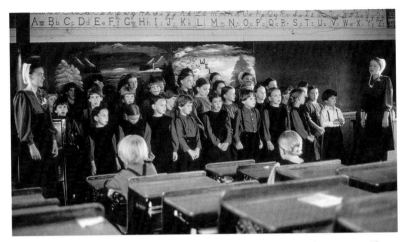

Students in Amish schools are typically taught by young single women. These students are practicing a song for a program for their parents; the teacher is on the right and the teacher's aide is at left.

teachers. A Christian song and a Scripture reading may open the school day, but religion is not taught in a formal way. Reading, spelling, writing, and math are the basic subjects. Science is not taught. Most textbooks are obtained from Amish publishers.

Regulations for attendance are stipulated by each state, and the quality of instruction varies by subgroup and region. In some communities, Amish pupils score well on standardized achievement tests. But the real test of Amish schools is not how they compare with high-tech suburban schools but how well they prepare Amish youth for success in Amish culture. Using that standard, Amish schools play an important role in passing on Amish values, developing friendships, and limiting exposure to the outside world. The schools contribute to the vigor and vitality of Amish life.

YOUTH AND RUMSPRINGA

Amish youth eagerly await their sixteenth birthday, the traditional age when they begin *Rumspringa*, a time of "running around." Before then, their peer relations mostly occur within the context of family activities. During *Rumspringa*, youth spend more time with their peers on weekends and may begin dating. A young man may take a young woman home in his buggy after a singing or a youth group picnic. *Rumspringa* ends at marriage, which usually occurs between nineteen and twenty-five years of age.

In the larger settlements, teens typically join one of many youth groups, which may claim dozens of members. Each group has a nickname and an identity based on how compliant or rowdy it is. Small Amish settlements with just one or two church districts may have only one youth group. Teens who begin *Rumspringa* at the same time often become friends for life. In some areas, those who join a youth group the same year are called a "buddy bunch."

Rumspringa is a moment of freedom when youth are suspended between two worlds: the control of their parents and the supervision of the church. Until they are baptized, they technically are not under the authority and rules of the church. Even so, many youth adhere to traditional Amish behavior.

It's true that some Amish young people flirt with worldliness by driving cars, watching television, being on social media, and listening to popular music, as well as by wearing English clothing, going to movies, hanging out in bars, and in some cases, using alcohol and drugs. The rowdier groups sometimes hold all-night parties that feature Amish bands with electric guitars, dancing, and alcohol. It's not unusual for some youth in more progressive communities to have smartphones and use various types of social media.

Parents worry about which group their youth will join, because the choice will influence the child's teen and adult behavior. But even most of the wilder youth eventually stop flirting with the world and join the church. Historically, youth groups had very little adult supervision. In recent years, more communities have adult supervisors to promote wholesome social and religious activities.

Age sixteen heralds the beginning of *Rumspringa*, or "running around," for Amish youth. Friends who join a youth group in the same year are often called a "buddy bunch." This buddy bunch is sharing stories before a Sunday evening singing.

For many Amish youth, *Rumspringa* means spending free time with friends on evenings and weekends engaged in activities such as playing volleyball.

Although some youth engage in wild activities, to the dismay of their elders, many others behave in traditional ways. Few go away to live in cities. Contrary to popular stereotype, the overwhelming majority of *Rumspringa*-age youth live at home and simply spend free time during evenings and weekends socializing with their peers. Youth activities may include playing volleyball or ice hockey, swimming, going on picnics, hiking at a state park, or attending large barn parties. The most typical gatherings are "singings," in which groups gather in a home and sing for several hours, followed by a time of socializing and food.

At first glance, rowdy teenage years appear as a tatter on the quilt of Amish culture. Experimenting with the world, however, can serve as a social immunization that strengthens their resistance later. A fling with worldliness reminds Amish youth that they have a choice regarding church membership. Still, Amish socialization is a powerful funnel toward church membership. Knowing that they had a choice may strengthen their willingness to obey church standards after they join. So any "wild oats" sown during *Rumspringa* may actually serve to strengthen the authority of the church in the long run.

MARRIAGE AND FAMILY

Church and family are the primary social units of Amish society. Young people move into adulthood early and usually marry by their early twenties. Marriages are not prearranged, but both bride and groom must be baptized members of the Amish church before marriage. They usually come from subgroups with similar practices but typically are not from the same church district. In rare cases a bride or groom may have grown up English and joined the Amish. Since divorce is forbidden, marriage is permanent.

Daylong weddings are festive moments of celebration in Amish society. The ceremony follows a lengthy church service, held on a weekday at the home of the bride or a close relative. Several hundred guests join the festivities, which often include a lunch and an evening meal.

The tables in this basement are set for a wedding reception. Amish weddings often include both a noon and evening meal for several hundred guests. In some communities, families rent trailers with kitchen facilities designed to serve large groups.

Amish couples, on the average, have about seven children, and in the most traditional groups, ten or more. Most families do not use artificial birth control unless advised by a physician for health reasons; however, some do use natural methods of family planning. Some babies are born in hospitals, but most greet the world in a birthing clinic or at home, under the supervision of a physician or a midwife.

Amish families reflect traditional gender roles, in which the man serves as the spiritual head of the home. He is seen as responsible for its spiritual welfare and matters related to the church and the outside world. Women often hold considerable sway in family and parenting matters. Quipped one husband, "I'm more afraid of my wife than my bishop." Another man described marital roles in this way: "The wife is not a servant; she is the queen, and the husband is the king."

Growth of Amish church districts, 1951–2021

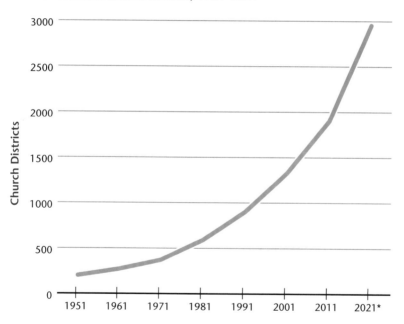

The number of Amish districts has grown exponentially since the 1950s because of large families and strong retention rates.

estimated based on current growth

Most Amish couples begin having children soon after they are married. It is not unusual for young married women to have several children by their mid-twenties.

As in most families, gender roles in Amish marriages vary by personality. When husbands work at home, spouses often share some roles. Women assist in the barn, shop, or field; men help in the garden, greenhouse, or around the house. Wives rarely hold full-time jobs outside the family when their children are young, although some operate small businesses from their home.

Networks of extended families provide a strong sense of identity in Amish society. The extended family system is muscular and significant. The typical Amish person has more than two dozen aunts and uncles and more than seventy-five first cousins, many of whom live nearby. The family provides a dense web of social support from cradle to grave. For instance, two or three relatives often assist a family during the arrival of a new baby. Adult sisters may gather once a month for a "sisters' day," a work frolic that blends chores and fun while women harvest vegetables, clean house, or make quilts. Family members help each other during a crisis or difficulty such as a fire, flood, or death.

Because families are so large and names are similar, many people have a nickname related to a special trait, or one that shows their family connection. "Horseradish Jake" may refer to someone who raises horseradish, or who eats a lot of it. A person named Sara may be known as "Ben's Hannah's Sara," referring to her grandfather and mother. The large Amish community near Lancaster, Pennsylvania, has more than one hundred women named Mary Stoltzfus and at least ninety Katie Stoltzfuses.

Extended family undergirds the elderly. The Amish do not operate retirement homes. The elderly normally live in a *Grossdawdy Haus*, a small adjacent "grandfather" house, or apartment, at the home of one of their children. Some grandparents have more than eighty grandchildren and two hundred great-grandchildren. Esteemed for their wisdom, the elderly find meaning and dignity as they assist their adult children. And surrounded by droves of grandchildren, they pass on the wisdom of Amish ways to the rising generation. Amish people typically die at home. More progressive communities accept hospice service from outside caregivers.

FOOD AND HEALTH

Making sweeping generalizations about all Amish families is risky—with one exception. That exception is gardens. Regardless of where they live or what they do, Amish people have bountiful gardens. Even so, many staples—sugar, flour, cereal, coffee, yogurt, ice cream, pretzels, and chips—are purchased at retail stores, including large chains. Some families also rely on store-bought bread, instant pudding, instant drink mixes, commercial snack foods, and canned soups. Amish stores sell bulk quantities of commercially processed cereals, canned fruits, and noodles, among many other items.

Although progressive Amish families purchase many staples and prepared foods, they still rely heavily on gardens and home-preserved foods. Many families butcher their own beef or pork. Non-farmers may arrange to receive fresh meat from friends who butcher or from an Amish-owned butcher shop.

The food prepared by Amish cooks varies by region. In eastern Pennsylvania, families enjoy regional specialties such as shoofly pie, sauerkraut, and scrapple, which is ground pork and beef combined with flour and cornmeal. Regardless of the regional fare, Amish foods are preserved and prepared in volume to feed large families and sizable numbers of visitors.

Because Amish homes don't have electricity, canning is the customary way of preserving food. It is not uncommon for a family to can large amounts, such as 150 quarts of applesauce, 100 quarts of peaches, and similar amounts of pears, grape juice, or other local fruits. Some families can as many as 50 quarts of tomato sauce for making homemade pizza throughout the year. A family may bake three dozen pies for the fellowship meal after the church service at their home. And a twelve-year-old girl may carry the weekly responsibility of baking a dozen loaves of bread for her family. Other families buy their bread at the store. For their Saturday evening meal, a family in a progressive group occasionally

Fresh tomatoes straight from the garden are a staple in summer. No matter the diversity of Amish life across different communities, gardens are a constant.

Right: Canning large amounts of produce in the summer and fall keeps food costs low and preserves the bounty of the garden for winter.

buys pizza from Pizza Hut and tops it off with store-bought ice cream. Popcorn and homemade ice cream are a typical Sunday evening snack in some families.

For frozen storage, some families rent freezer space at local stores or keep an electric deep freezer at the home of an English neighbor, whom they repay with produce from their garden or baked goods. Households in the most traditional subgroups have an icebox in their home for refrigeration.

The quality of healthcare varies greatly from community to community. Members of more isolated, conservative tribes might only see a doctor for an extreme emergency, such as a broken leg or a heart attack. More progressive-minded families consult a family doctor on a regular basis. Some families accept state-of-the-art medical technology for cardiac bypass surgery or even organ transplants.

In general, Amish families prefer natural treatments to chemical ones. Herbal tea is often preferred over an aspirin. Many people visit a chiropractor on a regular basis, because in Amish eyes, such doctors use more natural techniques than other medical doctors. A joke that I've heard many times in Amish circles poses this question: "How can you get an Amish man to the moon?" The answer: "Tell him there's a chiropractor on it, and he'll find a way to get there."

In more conservative families, high-tech fixes are sought only, if at all, after natural remedies fail. Some Amish patients seek relief through alternative, homeopathic treatments and from nontraditional practitioners. Ill people sometimes travel to unlicensed clinics in Mexico for treatment of cancer or other ailments. Natural remedies are viewed by many Amish as being closer to God's order in nature and therefore more trustworthy than complicated scientific interventions.

Most Amish people have an active lifestyle related to farming, construction work, gardening, or other manual work. High levels of physical activity enrich their health, as do garden vegetables. On the other hand, the diets of many families have saturated fats and salt aplenty, from things like sausage, bologna and other prepared sandwich meats, and deep-fried foods. For some, the effects of exercise and diet likely cancel each other out.

TILLERS OF THE SOIL

Ever since religious persecution pushed them into rural areas in Europe, the Amish have been tillers of the soil—and good ones. Their ties to the land have supported their common life and served as a cradle for the nurture of their children. Almost without exception, Amish parents say that the farm is the best place to raise children. It is a social seedbed, of sorts, in which children learn the virtues of responsibility, hard work, and teamwork.

"Good soil," said one leader, "makes a strong church where we can live together, worship together, and work together." On the farm—tilling the soil, cultivating crops, and caring for animals—one is closer to nature and to God.

With large families, Amish farming has always been a family affair. Church leaders have resisted large-scale mechanized farming that would steal work from children and erode family involvement. Using horse-drawn equipment is one way of resisting large, corporate-style farming. With a few exceptions, most farms are small family operations that use horses to pull machinery in the fields. Many farms have a tractor at the barn for high-power

Farm work is a family affair. Children assume many responsibilities at early ages. These children are hauling hay bales.

needs such as blowing silage to the top of silos, grinding grain, or pumping liquid manure.

For many years, Amish farms were small, diversified operations with a dozen milking cows, some chickens, and a few beef cattle. Although many continue this tradition, other Amish farmers have specialized in dairy and, in some cases, in poultry, goats, or hogs. Specialized Amish farms tend to be more mechanized, but always less so than their English neighbors. Farmers with more than twenty cows typically use mechanical milkers and bulk cooling tanks. The more traditional farmers milk by hand and ship their milk in old-fashioned cans to cheese plants.

Farm technology varies greatly among different Amish groups. More progressive groups use state-of-the-art hay balers adapted for horses.

Economic pressures have spurred more mechanization in many Amish communities.

Despite popular myths, not all Amish farmers practice organic farming. Many of them use insecticides, herbicides, and chemical fertilizers. A growing number are producing organic products, however, including vegetables, herbs, fruits, milk, cheese, yogurt, and beef. Some of these organic operations target upscale urban markets. A few farmers breed exotic game animals, such as buffalo, llamas, deer, quail, or pheasants. Others raise puppies for pet stores.

Economic pressures have prodded many families to seek non-farm employment. Even so, families frequently blend off-farm work with on-the-side farming, vegetable, and produce operations that involve their children. The most traditional groups have stubbornly resisted non-farm work and continue to cling to small family farms with little mechanization. Most families, regardless of their work, sing the virtues of rural life for keeping children in the Amish faith.

BUSINESS AND EMPLOYMENT

Despite their love of farming, the majority of Amish in many settlements have abandoned their plows. In some communities, the percentage of farmers has dipped below 15 percent. Yet in more isolated rural areas, about 75 percent of households remain engaged in full-time farming. The shift to non-farm work has wrought big changes in Amish society in recent decades. Even so, the Amish remain a distinctly rural people, living along country roads and on the outskirts of small towns and villages. Some families combine off-farm work with hobby farming. Three types of non-farm work flourish: small businesses, construction work, and employment in English factories.

Hundreds of small Amish-owned industries have sprung up in recent years. Most of these are small family operations with fewer than ten employees. With low overhead and ample family labor, these small businesses are productive and profitable. Annual sales in the larger ones may exceed $5 million. Enterprise ownership follows gender lines. Women are more likely to operate greenhouses, flower shops, fabric stores, food markets, bakeries, and roadside stands, whereas men typically own hardware stores, welding and machine shops, and woodworking or construction businesses.

A large portion of businesses produce wood products—household and outdoor furniture, upscale kitchens, gazebos, storage sheds, lawn ornaments, and doghouses, to name but a few of the hundreds. Other shops specialize in fabricating metal. Some of these build farm machinery, while others make products for outside English vendors and national retailers. Amish-owned stores that sell all sorts of hardware, dry goods, and food are also on the rise. Still other people operate delis and bakeries for dozens of farmers' markets that cater to outsiders living in suburban and urban areas.

Because Amish businesses do not use electricity from public utility lines, many of them power large machinery with pneumatic or hydraulic power from a diesel engine. This planer, run by hydraulic power, trims wood in an Amish furniture shop.

Construction work provides employment for many Amish men. In some settlements, dozens of construction crews may travel an hour or more to build homes and industrial buildings for non-Amish people. Amish-owned construction companies often hire some English employees who own and drive the transport vehicles for the Amish crews. Church rules governing the use of electrical tools are often relaxed at away-from-home construction sites. The most traditional tribes discourage construction work, because it increases the temptation to use technology and interact with the outside world.

In a few communities, most Amish men work in English-owned factories located in rural areas. In northern Indiana, for example, many Amish work in factories that build recreational vehicles.

Several hundred Amish may work in a factory, which creates, in effect, a small Amish world inside a high-tech industry. Fringe benefits, like medical insurance and Social Security that come with English employment, can tempt members to rely less on the church for mutual aid.

The growth of non-farm employment, both Amish and English, has brought new wealth to many Amish communities. Some elders worry that the new jobs bring too much "easy money and ready cash in pockets." In time, they say, these things will erode a work ethic and a frugality built on generations of farming.

Most Amish communities prefer small home-based shops rather than the "lunch pail" jobs that take fathers away from home. "What we're trying to do," said one young shop owner, "is to keep the family together."

THE PUZZLES OF TECHNOLOGY

Many people mistakenly assume that the Amish reject technology. In truth, they use a lot of technology, but they use it selectively. Certain technologies—televisions and computers, for instance—are rejected outright, but others are used selectively or modified to fit Amish purposes. I had never seen a 3-D printer until I walked into an Amish lantern shop in 2015. A dozen of them, running off a battery-powered inverter, had been programmed to create special couplings to connect LED lights to batteries for lighting Amish homes. Much state-of-the-art technology—gas grills, shop tools, camping equipment, and some farm equipment—is readily bought from English vendors without needing an Amish makeover. Amish mechanics adapt some commercial equipment to fit church guidelines, such as powering a 3-D printer from an inverter instead of tapping public grid electricity. They also create new machines to accommodate their cultural regulations.

Why do the Amish fear technology? If left untamed, certain technologies, they worry, will harm their community by disrupting traditions and bringing foreign values through mass media. They strike a distinction between sinfulness and worldliness. Technology is not considered evil in itself; "It's what it will do to the next generation," said one bishop. "A car is not immoral," he continued. "People who have cars aren't going to hell, but having a car would pull our community apart." In other words, no Bible verses prohibit cars; it's the community that matters!

The puzzles of Amish technology are perplexing to outsiders. Why would God frown on owning a riding lawnmower? What sense does it make to keep a tractor at the barn but not take it to the field? Is it not inconsistent, if not outright hypocritical, to refuse to own and operate a motor vehicle and yet hire rides and be driven around by outsiders? And what could the difference be between 12-volt electricity from batteries and 120-volt current from public utility lines?

These and many other practices may look silly to outsiders. Yet within the context of Amish history, these cultural compromises have helped to slow the pace of social change. Such adaptations reflect the Amish struggle to delicately balance tradition and progress without being swallowed up by contemporary life.

Leaders worry that using tractors for field work would lead to full-scale mechanization and the destruction of small family farms. Steel-wheeled tractors for high-power needs at the barn are preferred, to discourage using tractors on the road, which might, in time, lead to a car. (A few communities do permit tractors to be used in the field.) Likewise, riding mowers with rubber tires might also be a step toward the car. Horse-and-buggy transportation keeps the community anchored within a local geographical base. Cars, with their greater mobility, could pull the community apart. Although they prohibit owning motor vehicles, many Amish groups permit members to hire "taxis" driven by English neighbors to travel to distant weddings or funerals and to visit kin in far-flung settlements. And as already noted, some Amish entrepreneurs hire vans and trucks on a daily basis if their business requires considerable travel.

Most Amish groups forbid electricity from the public grid. "It's not the electricity that is so bad," said one member; "it's all the things we don't need that would come with it." Television, video games, computers, microwaves, and all sorts of modern conveniences might follow. Electricity from batteries is more local, controllable, and independent from the outside world. Batteries are

This home has a skylight. Refrigerators, stoves, and irons are often powered by natural or propane gas. An inverter that pulls current from a battery powers this electric fan. Many homes feature lovely Amish-made wood cabinetry.

used to power many things: lights on buggies, calculators, fans, flashlights, cash registers, copy machines, and in some progressive homes, LED lights. Solar energy is increasingly used to charge batteries, operate electric fences, and power small lights or household appliances. The most traditional subgroups forbid many of these technologies.

Amish manufacturing shops typically have a diesel engine that powers pneumatic (air) and hydraulic (oil) pumps to operate saws, grinders, sanders, lathes, and metal presses. Amish people with engineering acumen "Amishize" factory-made equipment by replacing its electric motors with pneumatic or hydraulic ones. Many shop owners claim that pneumatic or hydraulic power is, in fact, more efficient than electric power. In some homes, portable gasoline engines are used to power washing or sewing machines. Some of the more conservative groups prohibit pneumatic and hydraulic power.

Another piece of the puzzle draws a line between ownership and access. An Amish person employed in an English-owned factory has no restrictions on using its technology. Likewise, an Amish woman working as a secretary in a real estate office is allowed to operate the office computer but may not own one in her home. Similarly, an Amish man employed as a custodian of a motel may use a riding mower at work but not at home. The same access-but-not-ownership distinction also explains why riding in motor vehicles owned by outsiders is acceptable. This distinction gives Amish people access to a wide array of technology yet reminds them of its danger and protects their lives from being ensnared by it.

Telephones have been contentious since the first decade of the twentieth century when they first appeared in rural areas. For many years Amish churches prohibited them because of their connections to the outside world. Gradually, by the mid-twentieth century, more progressive tribes permitted a phone booth at the end of the farm lane, or some distance from the house, to make outgoing calls but keep incoming ones from disturbing family life. The growth of Amish businesses increased the adoption of phones. Well into the twenty-first century, the most traditional groups forbid ownership

Smartphones have filtered into some Amish communities, especially among teens and business owners, raising new questions about how to manage technology and prevent it from harming community and spiritual life.

of any phones, while the more progressive tribes permit them in the house. The acceptance of smartphones in some communities is usually determined district by district. This gigantic development for a separatist people provides easy access to the outside world but unlike a television it conveniently hides in a pocket.

From cars to phones, the Amish seek to master technology rather than become enslaved by it. They try to tame it, hoping to prevent harm to their family and community. In many ways they are more thoughtful and cautious about the impact of technology on social interaction than many of the rest of us, who eagerly gobble up all the gadgetry that energizes our high-tech society.

COMMUNITY RHYTHMS

A strong sense of community regulates the rhythms of Amish life. Face-to-face conversation in homes, on lawns, and in shops and barns provides the social glue of Amish society. Without big organizations, Amish life thrives in thick personal relationships that mix together neighborhood, family, church, work, and leisure. Despite many communal regulations, each individual is afforded respect and dignity. Church, family, and community are woven together seamlessly, unlike the sharp role segregation people face in mainstream society.

From birth to death, the Amish are surrounded by community. Here, members of a church district prepare a grave for a burial. Gravestones of similar size reflect humility and equality. Small stones show the graves of children.

One of the tenets of Amish faith is care and concern for others in the church. Members reach out to those in need, knowing that they too will receive care if a need arises. An injured farmer will find his crops harvested by neighbors with horse-drawn implements. After a flood or fire, the Amish community rallies quickly to clean up the debris and construct a new building. The traditional Amish barn raising illustrates the power of social capital as hundreds of people converge to erect a new structure in a day.

The habits of mutual aid stretch beyond floods and fires. Because the Amish reject commercial insurance, many communities have an informal aid plan to help members with major medical bills. Faced with large invoices or other exceptional needs, a family will find their local congregation taking a special offering for them, collected privately by the deacon in door-to-door visits. A public benefit auction or bake sale may also raise funds for members' special needs.

Many rhythms of community go beyond raising money. Parents gather to clean up local schools in preparation for the new academic year. Families who are moving can expect dozens of hands to carry furniture. Extended family members and neighbors gather in a work frolic to paint a house for newlyweds. Several adult siblings may meet monthly in a frolic for sewing, house cleaning, shelling peas, or canning tomatoes. Late winter auctions of

Amish frolics often blend work, fellowship, and fun. Women gather here in the sunroom of a contemporary Amish home for a quilting frolic.

household goods, farm equipment, and horses attract large crowds who come to socialize, eat, and catch up on the latest gossip. And of course, there are always quilting parties to attend. Visiting—which one member called "the national sport" of Amish life—bonds the community tightly together.

RECREATION AND LEISURE

Recreation in Amish life tends to focus on local activities involving nature. Without cars, and with chores galore, families are tied to the local community. Sledding, skating, swimming, fishing, and hunting provide breaks from the routines of work. Informal games of softball, corner ball, and volleyball have been longtime favorites in many Amish communities. Some children play with homemade toys and create their own games. Others use brightly colored plastic toys, tricycles, and Big Wheels.

Historically, endless farm chores underscored the importance of work, leaving little time for leisure. Indeed, pleasure and amusement were considered not only a waste of time but outright evil. Idleness, viewed as the devil's workshop, would lead to mischief or other vices. These attitudes still prevail in the more conservative communities, but among the non-farm Amish, recreational practices are changing.

Corner ball is a favorite game in some communities. The players on the outside circle try to hit the one from the opposing team in the center. This game is being played in a barnyard during an auction.

Families involved in business or factory work are finding more time for recreation. "We are more of a leisure people now," said one business owner. Another shop owner said, "We're businesspeople now, not just backwoods farmers, and sometimes we just need to get away." Several couples may travel together in a hired van to visit friends and relatives in out-of-state communities. Along the way, they may visit historic sites or stop at a state or national park. Large groups sometimes charter a bus to a historic village, a zoo, or a natural site. Family reunions and picnics are also popular times for visiting and relaxing.

Deer hunting is a major sport. Amish hunters may own or rent cabins in wooded areas. Other people may charter a boat to go deep sea fishing in the Atlantic or fish on one of the Great Lakes, depending on where they live. Archery is popular in some areas. Another favorite hobby is bird-watching. Adults who enjoy birding sometimes travel across the country to popular migration sites. Some young men go big game hunting in the Rocky Mountains for a week, equipped with guides and state-of-the-art guns and supplies. Other youth enjoy water-skiing or downhill skiing, depending on where they live.

Many Amish people enjoy outdoor sports such as hunting, fishing, and skating. This young man is unloading his boat for a fishing trip. Although some communities permit outboard motors for fishing, speedboats for water-skiing are discouraged.

During January and February each year, thousands of Amish people travel by chartered bus, van, or public transportation to Pinecraft, Florida. Pinecraft is a small Amish village with more than five hundred tiny houses and apartments on the outskirts of Sarasota. These snowbirds, who hail from many states, may stay for two weeks or the entire winter to enjoy the sun, the beach, and shuffleboard and especially to reconnect with friends they see once a year.

Recreation and travel is on the rise among more progressive families, but Amish leisure, for the most part, is not commercialized and remains entrenched in nature. Also, it is almost always community oriented, revolving around family and friends.

OUTSIDE CONNECTIONS

A day after the schoolhouse shooting at Nickel Mines, I received a call from a journalist asking, "How did the shooter get past security and onto the reservation?"

By now it should be clear that Amish people do not live on reservations or in cloistered communities enclosed by fences like those constructed at some tourist sites. They do believe in separation from the world, but that hedge of separation is largely cultural, not economic or geographic. All Amish people buy and sell products in the public marketplace, and their businesses operate in the mainstream capitalist economy. The owners of retail stores are in constant contact with outsiders. Moreover some Amish business owners participate in partnerships with non-Amish people. In a few settlements, many Amish people work in English-owned factories and interact with non-Amish employees every day.

The hedge of separation from the world is especially tall and thick for the most traditional Amish in isolated rural areas. These groups prohibit members from working for non-Amish employers and being a partner in an outside business. They also do not hire English drivers but rather require members to travel by horse and carriage and, in the case of long-distance travel, by public bus or train. These groups rarely participate in local civic fundraising or service projects. But even these separatist Amish have friendly relations with their nearby neighbors.

In more progressive Amish communities, strong friendships with non-Amish neighbors flourish as neighbors barter goods and help each other when special needs arise. And depending on the depth of trust, some Amish people use technology that they are not allowed to own but that is available in a neighboring English home, such as a food freezer, copy machine, or television. Some Amish sports fans may watch the World Series or the Super Bowl in an English neighbor's home. English "taxi" drivers who provide

Right: This Amish man is the assistant chief of a volunteer public fire company. He is watching preparations for a public benefit auction to support the fire company.

transportation on a regular basis for business owners and who drive Amish families to out-of-state weddings and funerals sometimes become close friends with their Amish clients. Even though few Amish people develop intimate relationships with outsiders or marry them, they still enjoy their friendship.

The Amish generally do not join public organizations or service clubs, such as Rotary, in the local community. In some settlements they are members of volunteer fire companies and emergency medical units. Even though the Amish are not allowed to drive fire vehicles, some companies could hardly survive without Amish, who far outnumber English firefighters and who often serve in leadership roles. In addition, Amish people help to organize and contribute valuable farm equipment, furniture, quilts, and other Amish-made products to sell in public auctions to raise funds for fire companies.

Benefit auctions or special meals organized by Amish people also support non-Amish organizations such as hospice, Habitat for Humanity, medical clinics, or other service organizations in their community. Amish people sometimes serve as blood donors for the Red Cross. It's also not unusual for Amish families to provide respite care or short-term foster care for, or even to adopt, non-Amish children under the auspices of the local children and youth services.

Many Amish groups participate in Amish or other Anabaptist disaster relief organizations that perform cleanup work and reconstruction for non-Amish people whose homes are devastated by tornadoes, flooding, or hurricanes. Through organizations such as Mennonite Disaster Service and Disaster Response Services, Amish people have traveled hundreds of miles in vans to clean up after storms such as Hurricane Katrina in Louisiana and Mississippi in 2005 and Hurricane Harvey in Texas in 2017, to name just two of many. Amish volunteers have also cleaned up and rebuilt after tornadoes and flooding in the Midwest.

GOVERNMENT TIES

Contrary to public misperception, the Amish do pay taxes. They pay state and federal income taxes, sales and real estate taxes, and public school taxes. In fact, in some states they pay for school twice: taxes for public schools and tuition for their private ones. They are exempt from paying Social Security taxes because they consider Social Security a form of insurance. The Amish believe that the Bible instructs them to care for the elderly and assist members who have special needs. To rely on commercial or government insurance would mock their belief that God will care for them through the church.

After a long struggle that involved fines and imprisonment, the U.S. Congress exempted the Amish from the Social Security system

In some areas, Amish people work in factories owned by non-Amish people, which raises issues about Social Security and workers' compensation taxes. This is the corporate headquarters of a garage door business in Ohio that employs Amish people in its manufacturing plants.

in 1966. Under this legislation they do not pay into or receive Social Security, Medicaid, or Medicare. However, English employers of Amish must pay Social Security for their Amish employees. Some states have also exempted Amish businesses from paying workers' compensation taxes for job-related injuries because the Amish consider that an insurance as well.

The Amish are taught to respect and pray for governing authorities according to biblical admonitions. When caught in a conflict between their conscience and civic law, however, they recite the Scripture that they should "obey God rather than men" (Acts 5:29). The intense persecution in Europe solidified their strong belief in the separation of church and state.

The Amish are pacifists and refuse to enter the armed forces. They generally avoid holding public office and political activism. They are, however, permitted to vote. The rate of voting is typically low unless a local issue is on the ballot. Two exceptions to that occurred in the presidential elections of 2004 and 2016. Some business owners and progressive-minded church members in eastern Pennsylvania, spurred on by their friendships with local politicians, actively promoted voting for the Republican candidates. Other Amish, citing a long-standing tradition of nonvoting, said, "We don't vote, but we pray Republican."

In recent years, numerous conflicts have pitted the Amish against the growing power of the state to regulate public behavior. The points of friction have included military service, education, Social Security, healthcare, property zoning, child labor, horseshoes chipping public roads, and red slow moving vehicle signs. Clashes tend to arise when the Amish move into new communities unfamiliar with their practices. One perennial skirmish involves horse droppings in small towns. This has led numerous municipal leaders to propose the use of diapers on horses.

To cope with the growing regulations that pricked their conscience, the Amish formed a national steering committee in 1967 with representatives in various states to work with public legislators when issues arise. All things considered, the Amish have fared rather well in a political system that respects and protects their freedom of religious expression.

AMISH WISDOM

From an outsider's perspective, it may appear that much of Amish life is about "giving up": giving up what you want, yielding to the community, and having one's individual freedom thwarted at every turn.

That's not how it felt to a ten-year-old Amish boy, who told me one day, "I'm so glad that I'm not English."

"Why?" I asked.

"Because I don't have to ride in a school bus like they do. I can just walk to school with my friends. And because my school stops at eighth grade, I can soon get a job." This young man, strong within his Amish identity and content within his birthright community, enthusiastically rated his upbringing higher than that of the outside world. His family wasn't anti-education. In fact, his eighth-grade-educated father had a library of about a thousand books, many of them on U.S. and world history.

Many of us who are not Amish are fascinated by a community that has found a way to preserve a strong sense of meaning, identity, and belonging—values that are often trampled underfoot by our hyper-paced world. What can we learn from our Amish neighbors who have crafted such a different life than most of us have?

Left: An Amish life is one lived within limits, which the Amish believe leads to true contentment. Humility, simplicity, community, and self-denial are prime virtues.

The Amish community is not perfect. Like other humans, Amish hearts sometimes throb with greed, jealousy, and anger. Parents worry about their children, and some youth rebel as in other societies. Although divorce is forbidden, marriages sometimes sour. Occasionally, some leaders abuse their power. There are also sporadic cases of sexual abuse reported. Disagreements sometimes debilitate congregational life and force communion to be postponed until harmony is restored. "We are not perfect," said one Amish man. "We have our own set of problems." Added a grandmother, "We have our good ones and our bad ones, just like anyone else."

Visiting with friends and family, sometimes on the front porch, remains a priority of Amish life.

Despite the blemishes, the Amish have developed a remarkable society. With little government aid, they provide care and dignity for their members. Apart from occasional arrests for alcohol or drug abuse among their youth, the Amish have avoided many of the blights of modern life. They have few in prison, and virtually no one is homeless, unemployed, or living on government subsidies. All things considered, they have created a rather humane society without high school, professional training, or high-tech accessories.

We can learn many things from our Amish neighbors, but several slivers of wisdom stand out. First, their respect for tradition underscores the importance of communal wisdom. Rather than turn to individual intellect and personal experience for authority, the Amish garner historical wisdom from their cultural reservoir. The combined wisdom of the community, they believe, is more reliable than the rational speculations of even a well-trained individual.

Second, they consider the welfare of the church community to be more important than individual freedom. Yielding selfish desires to the will of the church, they believe, brings deep meaning and purpose to life. In their eyes, pride and individualism are destructive. Humility, self-denial, and obedience to the community bring contentment and joy in the long run.

Third, the Amish have learned the importance of taming technology so that it serves, rather than controls, their community. Like few other groups, they have had the courage and tenacity to tackle the powerful forces of technology in order to preserve their traditional way of life. Ironically, they probably spend more time thinking about the human impact of technology than do most Americans.

Fourth, apart from large families, the Amish emphasize the importance of small-scale, informal social relations. "Bigness ruins everything," said one Amish carpenter. Schools are small, church districts are limited by the size of homes, and the church restrains the size of businesses. Intimate, face-to-face relationships add dignity and respect to human interaction.

The Amish have learned to live with limits. Indeed, they would argue that setting and respecting limits on almost everything is one of the foundations of wisdom. Limits, for the Amish, are a necessary requirement for human happiness. Without limits, individuals become arrogant, conceited, and self-destructive. And although restraints may appear to stifle individual freedom, they may in fact grant greater dignity and security to the individual than the endless choices and rotating options of modern life. A respect for limits builds community, brings belonging, and shapes identity— three important keys to satisfaction and happiness.

The Amish may enchant us at first glance, but a closer inspection shows that some of their values challenge our cherished views. We flinch from their conformity to plain dress and their limits on technology. Moreover, their rejection of college, not to mention high school, dismays us. Many Amish practices fly in the face of prized contemporary virtues, such as diversity, choice, gender equality, progress, and global awareness. Still, we find ourselves drawn to a people who spurn some of the cardinal values of modern life.

In some ways, the Amish trouble us, even torment us. Living without advanced technology, higher education, the latest fashions, and unfettered freedom, they seem to be just as happy—if not happier—than the rest of us. If joy is rooted in tradition and community, what choices face us? If contentment is found within limits and humility, how shall we then live?

Resources

Hurst, Charles E. and David L. McConnell. *An Amish Paradox: Diversity and Change in the World's Largest Amish Community*. Baltimore: Johns Hopkins University Press, 2010.

Johnson-Weiner, Karen M. *New York Amish: Life in the Plain Communities of the Empire State*. 2nd ed. Ithaca, NY: Cornell University Press, 2017.

Kraybill, Donald B. *The Riddle of Amish Culture*. 2nd ed. Baltimore: Johns Hopkins University Press, 2001.

Kraybill, Donald B., Karen Johnson-Weiner, and Steven M. Nolt. *The Amish*. Baltimore: Johns Hopkins University Press, 2013.

Kraybill, Donald B., Steven M. Nolt, and David Weaver-Zercher. *Amish Grace: How Forgiveness Transcended Tragedy*. San Francisco: Jossey-Bass, 2007.

———. *The Amish Way: Patient Faith in a Perilous World*. San Francisco: Jossey-Bass, 2010.

Nolt, Steven M. *The Amish: A Concise Introduction*. Baltimore: Johns Hopkins University Press, 2016.

———. *A History of the Amish*. 3rd ed. New York: Good Books, 2016.

Smucker, Janneken. *Amish Quilts: Crafting an American Icon*. Baltimore: Johns Hopkins University Press, 2013.

Stevick, Richard. *Growing Up Amish: The Rumspringa Years*. 2nd ed. Baltimore: Johns Hopkins University Press, 2014.

Umble, Diane Zimmerman and David Weaver-Zercher, eds. *The Amish and the Media*. Baltimore: John Hopkins University Press, 2008.

Amish Studies at Elizabethtown College is the premier academic site for Amish-related information, including an annual update on Amish demographics. Visit groups.etown.edu/amishstudies.

Amish America is an excellent and frequently updated resource for all things Amish. Visit AmishAmerica.com.

The Amish is a comprehensive film featuring authentic Amish voices explaining their way of life. Produced by American Experience, it was widely shown on PBS. To view or purchase *The Amish*, visit pbs.org/wgbh/americanexperience/films/the-amish.

THE AUTHOR

D onald B. Kraybill is internationally recognized for his scholarship on Anabaptist groups. His books, research, and commentary have been featured in national and worldwide media, including the *New York Times*, *Washington Post*, *The Guardian*, NPR, CNN, and NBC. He is distinguished college professor and senior fellow emeritus at the Young Center for Anabaptist and Pietist Studies at Elizabethtown College. Kraybill is the author, coauthor, or editor of many books, including *Amish Grace*, *The Amish Way*, *Renegade Amish*, and *The Riddle of Amish Culture*.